Murphy Enterprise Solutions

Presents

Big City Nights
The Biography of the Legendary Cisero Murphy

by

Tyriek A. Murphy, MPA

Illustrations by: Murphy Enterprise Solutions

DORRANCE
PUBLISHING CO
EST. 1920
PITTSBURGH, PENNSYLVANIA 15238

Dorrance Publishing Co
585 Alpha Drive
Suite 103
Pittsburgh, PA 15238
Visit our website at *www.dorrancebookstore.com*

ISBN: 978-1-4809-4784-9
eISBN: 978-1-4809-4807-5

Abstract

This book you're about to embark upon is a detailed depiction of a dramatically dynamic individual, whose family ancestry dates back to the late nineteenth century, determined to diversify a sports area dedicated and dominated by Caucasians during the mid twentieth century. This essential gentleman has repeatedly set records that are still intact today, in the twenty-first century. Whether locally, nationally, or internationally, this man displayed the utmost professionalism during times of devastation derived from racial discrimination. Despite the dangerous deviations, he dissected his way through in life; he always found the directional path to overcome the odds. His breakthrough ultimately paved the way for other diverse players and, essentially, women to partake in the pastime. As a result, and considered by many to be the "Jackie Robinson" of the billiards world, this iconic figure holds the record for being the only Black American world title winner and Hall of Fame inductee in professional billiards history. Enjoy this literature piece about the Legendary Cisero Murphy.

Disclaimer

In accordance within any local, state, and/or Federal laws, this literary work was completed with full verbal and/or written consent from essential parties with first account knowledge associated with the accurate depiction of Murphy's life. Any other individual(s) not mentioned, particularly by name, in this book was done specifically with the goal of minimizing any litigation.

Acknowledgments

Special thanks are in order to the following:

To: Cisero S. Murphy, my grandfather, for accomplishing goals through hard work and determination in a world ready to write him off based upon his complexion color. In addition, for believing in my greatness as his grandfather did his capabilities.

To: Janie Mae Kearse, my grandmother, for giving me the insight to her connection with Cisero and for being a foundational facet of my childhood.

To: Cisero K. Murphy, Jr., my father, for depicting to me the type of individual he is.

To: Renee F. Humphrey, my mother, for undoubtedly being the reason my grandfather's prophecy transpired.

To: Christalee Kearse, my aunt, for being one of Janie's strong and supportive sisters.

To: James Thomas, Joseph Armstrong, Lee Bynum, and William Shoates, for being great supporters and friends of Cisero for decades.

To: David Sapolis, Cisero's Mentee, for sharing your knowledge and experiences with Cisero.

To: All professional billiards tournaments in which Cisero played, for giving my grandfather the opportunity to partake in a sport not accustomed to Black American engagement.

To: Billiards Congress of America, for ultimately realizing that the sport of billiards had a special player in its midst and had proven to be one of a kind.

To: The Immediate Community of Bedford Stuyvesant, for those who supported Cisero from the sunny days, through the dark days, and to the sunny days again—especially to the neighbors on Hancock Street.

Lastly,
To: You, the reader, for acquiring this literary piece and taking the necessary step forward to ensuring that the information regarding Cisero S. Murphy is clearly understood, accurate, and most essentially, to enlighten those whom you may come across, in your life journey, to what Cisero S. Murphy meant, not just to the Black American existence, but entirely to society.

Contents

Chapter 1

The Humble Beginnings of The Murphy Family

In the year 1876, the first Cisero Murphy was born in the township of Vanceboro, North Carolina. His parents had been slaves. They lived and worked on a farm within the same city and state. Although Cisero wasn't born during the time his parents were slaves, he was told many stories by his parents about the pain and suffering they encountered during slavery. As young Cisero was growing up, he didn't attend school. Instead, he was taught two factors; they were, firstly, how to operate and sustain the farm, and lastly, his attending Sunday morning fellowship services with the community.

Cisero was in his early teens when his father suffered a heart attack. The medical incident prohibited him from continuing his normal daily activities. Naturally, Cisero started working extra hours every day in the fields to ensure the work wouldn't build up. At the end of each day, Cisero would give his father a detailed description of his daily activities, in which his father was very pleased. One day after Cisero provided the daily account, his father pointed out to him, in a weak voice,

"One day you will be the man of the house, and with that comes a lot of responsibilities. As the man of the house, you must be strong, not only for yourself, but for your family as well. Most importantly, you must be a man of integrity."

Those were the last words he spoke before falling into a deep sleep. Unbeknownst to Cisero, it would be his last conversation with his father.

The next day, as Cisero was working in the field, he heard his mother yell loudly, and he raced back to the house. Upon entering the house he saw his mother kneeling over his father, crying. Hearing her son approaching, she reached back for her son's hand and simultaneously conveyed, "He's gone; your father passed away!"

After hearing his mother say those words, he knelt down beside her and held her close, as they both cried. Cisero and his mother were devastated, but the love and support of the community helped them both deal with the hurt of losing a loved one. Cisero, however, in remembering his last conversation with his father, became the man of the house. He worked very hard to maintain the farm and provide for his mother. Every Sunday, Cisero would accompany his mother to the *Community Fellowship Service*. She had openly testified to how blessed she was to have a son like Cisero.

Chapter 2

It Is Time to Be a Man; a Murphy Man

However, as time passed, Cisero noticed that his mother was complaining more about having throbbing headaches. After seeing a doctor, it was determined that his mother had a bad case of hypertension. His mother would have to take some medication to help her with the hypertension, but most importantly, get rest. Cisero immediately started helping his mother with the house chores to ensure she'd have more time to rest. Regardless, every Sunday morning, she'd get up early to prepare and cook dinner before going to the *Community Fellowship Service* for worship. Although she wouldn't allow Cisero in her kitchen while she prepared Sunday's dinner, he would always stay close by to assist. She appreciated his unconditional support. One evening during dinner, Cisero confided in his mother his interest in a young teenaged girl. The female lived on the adjacent farm with her parents, and they also attended the same congregation. However, before he could even mention her name, his mother cut him off and asked, "Who, Harriette?" Cisero was completely taken by surprise. He had no idea his interest in Harriette was transparent. He sat his dinner fork down on the table and said, "Yes, mother; Harriette!" Once again, before he could continue, his mother interrupted. She asserted, "She is a wonderful young lady. You should invite her over for dinner one evening, so I could formally meet her."

Harriette Murphy

Cisero's mother was very happy her son was growing up into a fine young man. She knew his father would have shared the same feelings. Following his mother's advice, Cisero invited Harriette and her parents to Sunday dinner. Harriette and her parents were very delighted and accepted

Cisero's invitation. After service on the following Sunday, everyone headed to Cisero's house for dinner. Once inside the house, Cisero and Harriette's father sat in the living room and engaged in small talk while the women started setting the dining table. Once the table was set, everyone took their place. Cisero, however, hesitated, because this was the first time he sat at the table as the man of the house. Cisero asked, "Would everyone please join hands?" as he blessed the food.

During dinner, Cisero was very nervous, because he was expecting a rough line of questions from Harriette's parents. Surprisingly, everyone just enjoyed their meal with small talk and laughter. After the main course was served, Cisero's mother served desert in the living room by the fire-place. Once the desert was finished, the women returned to the dining room to clear off the table, thus leaving the men in the living room. Harriette's father took this opportunity to have a man-to-man conversation with young Cisero concerning his true intentions as they related to his daughter. Cisero looked Harriette's father directly in his eyes, in a mature tune, and expressed his unwavering feelings for Harriette and his intention to ask for Harriette's hand in marriage. Harriette's father, at first, was skeptical of Cisero, but dismissed any doubts after hearing such a mature response. At this point, Harriette's father was very proud of this young man and of his upbringing. He insisted, "As I listen to you speak, the more I'm reminded of your father's legacy. He was a man of integrity, and very well respected in the community. Most essentially, he was one of my closest friends for years prior to his passing."

He approached Cisero while simultaneously extending his right hand to offer a warm handshake of approval, to which Cisero gladly accepted. The men, being completely satisfied with their manly conversation, conversed for a few more minutes before the women returned to the living room in laughter. As Harriette and her parents were putting on their coats, they each expressed their appreciation for such a wonderful and memorable evening. They all gave each other a warm embrace before saying their goodbyes.

Once all of the guests were gone, Cisero turned to his mother, in a jubilant state, and thanked her for being such a gracious host, while simultaneously kissing on her cheek. His mother, unaware of the masculine conversation held with Harriette's father, in a joking manner said, "Wow, someone clearly had a good night!" which caused both of them to laugh. She then gave Cisero a warm embrace and said, "You are welcome, my son!" as they both journeyed toward their rooms. Cisero turned around and noticed his mother leaning against the wall near her bedroom door. Cisero immediately approached his mother and helped her inside the room. Cisero's mother expressed to him that she was exhausted. Not taking any chances, he called the doctor. After the doctor's examination, it was ascertained her blood pressure was extremely high, and the cause of her dizzy spell. The doctor gave his mother medication to bring her blood pressure down. He ordered her to stay in bed for three days because her body was too weak. He further related that he would return to complete a follow-up inspection.

The next day, Cisero informed Harriette and her family of what happened to his mother. Harriette and her parents immediately offered their assistance. Harriette and her mother came by the house every day to cook and attend to his mother while Cisero and Harriette's father worked together to maintain both farms. Cisero was very grateful for their unwavering support. On the third day, the doctor returned to check her condition. After conducting his examination, he told Cisero that his mother's body was regaining strength. He further explained to Cisero that his mother had suffered a mild stroke. If she didn't change her daily activities, she could suffer another stroke. The doctor asked, "Do you know if your mother stresses or worries a lot?"

Cisero replied, "My mother didn't fully overcome the death of my father. Once in a while, she'll sit in her room just staring out the window for hours."

The doctor jotted down Cisero's comments and reiterated his earlier medical advice. Adding that he'd like to give her something to help with the stressing. He believed her stress was the cause of her constant headaches, and contributed it to the mild stroke she endured. Before departure, the doctor mentioned he'd do a couple progress follow-ups to monitor how his mother was responding to the medication. Cisero walked the doctor to the front door and thanked him for his service.

Upon returning to his mother's bedroom, she motioned for him to come over and sit beside her. Her eyes full of tears, she reached for her son's hand and thanked him for his quick thinking, which contributed to saving her life. Cisero embraced his mother and replied, "You are welcome!" He kissed her on the forehead and instructed her to get some rest. As Cisero closed his mother's bedroom door, he heard noise coming from the kitchen. Harriette was in the kitchen preparing something to eat for his mother. Cisero approached her from behind and kissed her lightly on her cheek. Harriette turned around and asked, "How is your mother doing?" Cisero gave her a full progress report, as he sat down at the table to enjoy the meal she'd prepared for him. As he was eating, Harriette took a tray of food to his mother's bedroom. As Cisero's mother was eating, Harriette started cleaning her room, while engaging her in small talk. When Harriette was finish cleaning the room, she thanked Harriette for her steadfast support. Harriette sat down on the bed beside her, and said, "You are welcome, Mom!"

Cisero's mother gently pushed Harriette away with excitement in her voice, and asked, "Are you expecting?"

Harriette, caught off guard, replied, "No, I am not! I called you mom because I see you and respect you as a mother figure." Cisero's mother was so pleased that she reached for Harriette to give her a warm and passionate hug, signifying a welcome to the family. Harriette, fully joyful, stood up, and saying, "Okay, you have to get some rest now. I will be back shortly to check on you, okay, Mom?"

They both looked at each other and smiled. Harriette picked up the tray and returned to the kitchen. Once in the kitchen, she noticed Cisero from the window working on the farm. She started to prepare supper. After the meal was done, Harriette returned to Cisero's mother's bedroom where they both engaged in more conversation and laughter. A little while later, Cisero walked into his mother's bedroom and was very happy to see Harriette and his mother bonding. A short time later, Cisero escorted Harriette home and thanked her for helping his mother.

A few days later, the doctor returned to conduct a progress follow-up with Cisero's mother. The doctor was very pleased to see that the medication was helping and there were no side effects occurring. Essentially, he was completely satisfied that Cisero's mother had regained her body strength, and he released her from bed rest. However, the doctor warned Cisero's mother she still had to refrain from strenuous and stressful activities. He further related that she needed to maintain a low sodium diet and start a light workout routine. Lastly, the doctor instructed her to take frequent periods of relaxation. He reiterated that following his advice should help decrease any chances of her having another stroke. Cisero and his mother thanked the doctor for his due diligence before he departed.

Chapter 3

The Murphy Expansion

The following Sunday, Cisero's mother made a big dinner to show her appreciation for Harriette and her parents' relentless support. As the years passed by, Cisero's mother noticed that Harriette and her son had built an unbreakable bond. In May of 1898, Cisero, twenty-two years old, and Harriette, nineteen years old, got married in their place of worship. The decision was made to live with Cisero's mother on the farm, as a result of her failing health condition. Naturally, Cisero's mother was elated at their decision to reside with her. She didn't want to live in the enormous house alone. She was happy that God allowed her to witness her son's marriage to his beautiful wife, whom she admired dearly. She began to instruct Harriette on how to prepare Cisero's favorite meals. Harriette and Cisero's mother would talk about the essential facets of family and its role. In one of the many conversations, Cisero's mother confided to Harriette that she was hoping one day to give birth to a beautiful baby girl. The untimely death of her husband altered the possibility. She further related to Harriette, "God is a giving God, by which your marriage to my son is God's way of providing me a beautiful baby girl."

Harriette, surprised and speechless, began a perpetual flow of tears. She embraced Cisero's mother with a hug and kiss while simultaneously uttering, "Thank you!"

Later that evening, Cisero finished working on the farm, came home, and noticed that Harriette was in a jubilant manner. He smiled then asked,

"What has you so excited, honey?" She related to him the conversation between his mother and herself. Cisero, pleased to hear about their interaction, replied, "She is an amazing person!" Harriette concurred. As the weeks passed by, Harriette enjoyed the wisdom Cisero's mother bestowed upon her. However, to Harriette, it seemed as if she was retiring and passing the torch. Harriette's notion was confirmed when Cisero's mother had another stroke and passed away. Cisero and Harriette were devastated. He was very grateful for the love and support he'd received from his wife, her parents, and the community. It was quite a while before Cisero and Harriette were able to overcome the grief of her death.

Incidentally, on Friday, April 8, 1903, Cisero and Harriette became the proud parents of Herbert Murphy. In September 1907, Harriette gave birth to Mary Murphy. Cisero and Harriette taught their children how to work and maintain the farm, just as Cisero was educated by his father. On Sundays, the family would attend *Community Fellowship Service*. It was during one of these sessions that Herbert met Eva Campbell.

Herbert and Eva Murphy

Father Campbell (Eva's Dad)

Campbell was born on Sunday, December 25, 1909, in Craven County, North Carolina. Subsequently, the two got married in 1927. The ceremony took place in Campbell's birth location of Craven, NC. After the wedding, Herbert and Eva relocated to New Bern, North Carolina, because he obtained an on-site living job maintaining a farm located at 720A West Street. On Monday, November 17, 1928, Herbert and Eva became the parents of a baby girl. In 1930, the couple had James Murphy. Cisero and Harriette were ecstatic with Herbert and Eva for giving them two lovely grandchildren. Mary was equally elated about her niece and nephew, and called them her two little pearls, to which Harriette replied, "Okay, Aunt Pearly!" Mary, so excited, accepted the nickname given by her mother.

In 1931, Mary, age twenty-four, decided to relocate to Brooklyn, New York. Her parents, not wanting her to move so far away, supported her decision. Once in New York, Mary secured an apartment located at 1360 Fulton Street, Brooklyn, NY, and procured employment at a factory nearby.

Cisero and Harriette were pleased to know that both of their children were doing well in life, in their own right. Herbert and Eva shared the same pleasure and were amused by her new nickname.

Chapter 4

The Birth of a Legend

As the months passed, Herbert and Eva had a conversation about increasing their family, by which they decided to have one more child and wait a couple of years before having another. Accordingly, in 1933, Eva gave birth to their third child, a second boy child. Herbert, being a proud father, decided to name his son Herbert Murphy Jr. Cisero and Harriette, always supportive, couldn't wait to embrace their new grandchild. Two years later, on October 2, 1935, Eva gave birth to their fourth child. Herbert and Eva honored his father by naming the baby boy Cisero S. Murphy. When Herbert's dad learned of this, he was happy, and tears filled his eyes as he simultaneously thanked them both. As the elder Cisero walked over to the bed of young Cisero, he raised young Cisero into the air and depicted a prophesy of greatness for his grandson. He insisted, "Your name will be known in certain parts of the world, way before you ever get there!"

The elder Cisero applied a kiss to young Cisero's forehead and placed him back on the bed, then proceeded to play with the other grandchildren. Cisero and Harriette stayed for a couple of hours and then left to go home. Elated and exhausted from the day's events, they put the children to bed and retired for the night themselves.

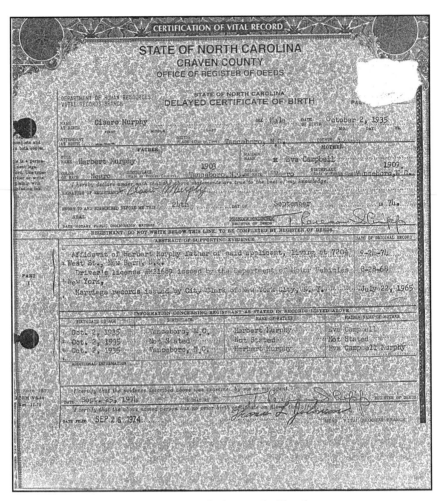

Cisero Murphy's proof of birth

Chapter 5

The Pursuit for a Better Life

As time passed, Herbert and Eva wanted more for their children. They wanted the kids to attend a good school, have a good job, a big house, get married, and have a family of their own. Herbert and Eva realized that changes needed to be made within their lives in order to achieve the bigger goals. Eva, with Herbert's blessing, found employment on another farm. Herbert called Mary in NY and elaborated that he wanted to relocate the family to NY, and asked for assistance. Mary agreed to help the family in any way possible. In 1937, Herbert and Eva decided to send their only daughter and young Cisero to live with his sister Mary. Herbert chose to keep James and Herbert Jr. to help on the farm.

For the next two and half years, Mary would travel back and forth from New York to North Carolina to allow the kids to spend time with their siblings and parents. Finally, in 1940, Herbert, Eva, and the two children moved to NY, reuniting with the other two kids, while all living in Mary's Brooklyn apartment. The family found an apartment on Gates Ave. However, not satisfied with the building conditions, Herbert secured another apartment located on Putnam Ave. in Brooklyn, NY, with a better state of affairs, and financially affordable. In 1941, Herbert and Eva enrolled Cisero, age six, and Herbert Jr., age eight, into Public School 44, located on Monroe Street in Brooklyn, NY. Their daughter, thirteen, and James, eleven, were enrolled into a local junior high school.

In 1942, Herbert Sr. was fortunate enough to obtain a government job within the *Works Progress Administration* (WPA). The finances Herbert earned at WPA allowed him to move the family into a larger apartment located on Marcy Ave in Brooklyn, NY. However, the kids were still in the same school district. A few months later, Herbert found a large three bedroom apartment for his family around the corner, on Lexington Ave, which became home for the next three years. Additionally, in 1945, the family size increased, and more space was needed. Herbert and Eva moved their family to a larger apartment located at 1342 Fulton Street in Brooklyn, NY. Since their new apartment was no longer in *Public School 44 School District*, Cisero and Herbert Jr. were transferred to *Public School 93* located at 31 New York Ave, Brooklyn, NY.

Herbert was very appeased with the way life was going. He wanted to do something special for his family. Herbert decided to buy a black-and-white television (TV). He loved a variety of sports. Herbert would sit in front of the TV on the weekends with his boys and watch sporting events. His daughter would frequently join in as well. Herbert, being closer to the boys, would take them to Kingston Park, located on Herkimer Street and Kingston Avenue, to play softball, basketball, and touch football. He also gave the boys lessons on self-defense and how to repair things within a house. Eva would teach the girls, at an early age, how to cook and maintain their home. After having a conversation with Herbert, Eva decided to obtain a job to provide extra financial support. A week later, Eva found employment within a Brooklyn factory called *College Donuts*.

Chapter 6

The Breaking Point

A year later, Herbert became ill and was unable to do the physical work required at WPA. He grew frustrated with his inability to provide for his family economically. This was the first time in his life he was fired from employment. Eva attempted to reassure him that matters would get better. However, Herbert felt embarrassed and felt as though he let the family down. For days, he would complain and release his frustration out on his wife. The pair would engage in verbal confrontations, especially after Herbert would consume alcoholic beverages. Eva would pray that matters would change for the better, particularly with her husband, because she grew increasingly tired of the abuse.

A week later, *College Donuts* announced they were hiring. Herbert applied for the job and a week later was hired. Eva thought that if her husband got a job, he would change those abusive ways; however, she was wrong. One evening after work, Herbert waited until the children were sleeping before confronting Eva. He accused her of being "too friendly" with the guys at work, and he didn't appreciate it. Eva denied his accusations and attempted to walk away. Herbert grabbed her by the arm, with enough force to spin her around, and emphasized, "You'd better not ever let me found out that you're disrespecting me with someone on that there job, or anywhere else!"

Eva was frightened of her husband. He'd become suspicious, very controlling, and she didn't want to live life that way. Moreover, Eva knew she couldn't take a day off from work without causing Herbert to notice. She waited until one of the children had a doctor's appointment in order to go file for a divorce.

One evening, Eva started feeling dizzy. She thought it was the result of the humidity in the air. Eva was transported to *St. John's Hospital* located at 480 Herkimer Street, Brooklyn, NY. After a complete examination, the doctor informed Eva of her pregnancy. The doctor further related that she needed to stay off her feet for long periods of time. He feared the dizziness would return, causing an unsafe medical event for herself and the unborn baby. Adhering to the medical advice, Eva decided to discontinue her employment at *College Donuts*. Everyone was elated about the news except Herbert. After the kids' bedtime, Herbert expressed some doubt, because he felt she was "friendly" enough to get pregnant by one of the colleagues at work. Eva was hurt that her husband would insinuate that she was unfaithful. Eva, with tears in her eyes, asserted, "I can't live like this anymore! You don't trust me and you think I've been unfaithful to you? To the point where you're denying your child, your unborn child? I'm going to pray for you!!"

Herbert didn't respond; he continued to get ready for bed. Eva, heated from the exchange between Herbert and herself, decided to stay up longer before going to bed.

The following morning, Eva's oldest daughter made breakfast for everyone. After breakfast, she had a conversation with Eva regarding helping the family's economic crisis. The next day, Eva's oldest daughter applied and was hired by *College Donuts*, where she would work the assembly line. Eva was proud to observe her oldest daughter starting her journey to independence. As for Herbert, he was happy, because now there was a second income to help with the bills.

A few months later, Eva gave birth to a handsome boy in *St. John's Hospital*, the couple's fourth child since relocating to New York. (The others being Alfred Murphy, Rosabelle Murphy, and Susana Murphy). Herbert, after viewing the baby, acknowledged that he was indeed the father. However, his love for Eva had seriously diminished beyond any point of recovery. When the *Kings County Supreme Court* granted Eva's divorce request, an official copy was served to Herbert while he was at work. Herbert was simultaneously surprised and embarrassed. It was in this moment that Herbert decided to leave New York and return to North Carolina. He gave his employer one week's notice and went home to pack his bags. He didn't want the kids to observe him leaving. The next morning, Herbert got up early to go collect his final check from *College Donuts* before his daughter started her shift. Herbert returned to the domicile, collected his belongings, and left without saying a word to Eva. When Eva's daughter came home from work, she found her mother holding the baby and crying. She asked, "What's wrong, Mother?" Eva told her the divorce was finalized, that her father had moved out and wouldn't be returning. Lost for words, Eva's daughter sat beside her and her sibling. Eva asserted, "I don't know how to tell the children their father left and won't be returning!"

Her daughter looked her in the eyes, and stated, "I will help you tell the children, okay? We'll do this together!!"

Eva was grateful for her support. Later that evening, Eva and the oldest daughter told the residual children the whole uncut story and how it would affect the family life. They reiterated the point of their father still loving them regardless to his non-existence within the family household. One of the children asked, "When will we see daddy again?"

Eva, with no definitive answer, replied, "As soon as he reestablishes himself, your father will be in touch!" Hearing those words put all the kids' tension at ease. However, life for them was never going to be the same. The daughter continued to work at *College Donuts* and help where she could. Meanwhile, Eva decided to apply for and obtain public assistance for the family.

Chapter 7

The Aftermath and Beyond

As time had gone by, Eva was adjusting to her new status as a single parent. One evening, Eva noticed that her oldest daughter was acting abnormal. Eva waited until the children went to bed to question her daughter. To Eva's surprise, she learned that her daughter had met a handsome young man by the name of Richard. They'd been secretly dating for approximately six months. Eva asked her daughter when she would meet him; she related that it would be very soon. A week later, Eva's oldest daughter invited Richard to the house to be formally introduced to her mother and siblings. The evening went well, and everyone enjoyed Richard's company. Richard was a sports lover, which allowed him to connect with the boys. At the end of the evening, Eva related to her daughter that he was a nice young man and that it was a pleasure meeting him. Eva gave her daughter a warm hug and kiss, and bid her a good night. Over a year later, Richard formally asked Eva for permission to marry her oldest daughter. Undoubtedly, Eva gave her blessing for their union. A short time thereafter, the couple was married and moved to the Flatbush section of Brooklyn, NY. However, Eva's daughter would return frequently to help with her siblings and/or family finances.

One weekend, Eva took her son, Cisero, with her food shopping at the local A&P supermarket. While she was shopping, she noticed that Cisero was conversing with a young girl. The adolescent girl lived in their building on the fourth floor. Eva continued to shop. Once finished, she approached the two of them. Eva handed Cisero some of the groceries bags while simultaneously greeting the young female. Eva asked, "What is your name?"

The little girl responded, "I'm Janie Kearse" (born Janie Mae Kearse in South Carolina in March of 1938).

Eva then asked, "Are you here with someone?"

Janie replied, "Yes, my mother, and here she comes." Eva looked in the direction Janie pointed and saw a lady approaching.

As the lady was near, she asked, "Is everything okay here?" Eva assured Janie's mother that there was no problem and introduced herself.

Janie's mother replied, "Okay. Hello, I'm Sylvia Kearse." Eva further related that she saw Janie and Cisero conversing for a while, and thought Janie was alone.

Sylvia replied, "No, I am here!" Sylvia further claimed to recognize Cisero from the school, *Public School 93*, where her children attended and where she was employed. Sylvia also stated she knew Cisero lived on the sixth floor in the same building. Eva and Sylvia were elated to know both were being observant. This was the first of many laughs shared among the two ladies. They all left the supermarket walking toward their residence located at 1342 Fulton Street, Brooklyn, NY. Along the way, Eva asked Sylvia, "So, how long have you been living here?"

Sylvia replied, "Since 1940, when our family moved here from South Carolina." Eva shared how her family came from North Carolina. Once they reached their building and proceeded inside, Sylvia sent Janie to get paper and a pen to exchange phone numbers with Eva. After the exchange of information, Eva and Cisero headed to their apartment.

Naturally, as time elapsed, Eva and her family became very close with Sylvia and her family. Since all the children attended *Public School 93*, they all walked together to and from school. Frequently, Cisero would visit Janie at home. He spent so much time there that Sylvia considered him to be her son. When Cisero observed how affectionate Janie's father was to her, he would be reminded how much he missed his father. Cisero was frustrated because of his parents' divorce. Cisero, in one of many conversations, expressed to Janie his desire to join a boxing gym to relieve some stress, and perhaps, if successful, win a title.

PAL Wynn Center

Therefore, with Eva's permission, Cisero joined *Police Athletic League Wynn Center* (PAL) located on Gates Avenue in Brooklyn, NY. As a result of joining the PAL, Cisero realized he wouldn't be able to wait for Janie after school. Cisero would rush home, change into workout clothes, grab his gym bag, and power walk or jog the eight blocks on Marcy Avenue until he reached the PAL. Cisero's impetuosity was to ensure he get to the PAL to sign out the equipment and work on the punching bag. Cisero would return home after seven o'clock in the evening during weekdays. He was only able to visit Janie on the weekends.

Chapter 8

The Element of a Competitor

In February 1949, Cisero graduated from *Public School 93*. His school records were transferred to *George Westinghouse High School*. Cisero was instructed to report there for the first day of school. Cisero, after some time had passed, was subsequently transferred to *Boy's High School* located on Marcy Avenue. After completing his freshman and sophomore years, Cisero decided that he didn't want to continue with his education and left the school system.

Cisero Murphy's official school transcript

Cisero immediately found a job as an auto mechanic and began helping with the family finances. He budgeted a portion of his income to purchase items for his boxing lessons. For years, Cisero would go to work and to the PAL to train. However, one summer evening, Cisero arrived late and was unable to sign out any boxing equipment. Frustrated with himself, he decided to stay and partake in other activities within the PAL. Having never gone to the second floor, Cisero made the choice to explore the upstairs section. Once upstairs, he saw a few gentlemen standing near a pool table. Since the table wasn't in use by the men, Cisero walked over to it and picked up a stick to play. This was the first time Cisero had ever held a pool stick. He took several attempts to shoot the ball inside the pocket holes on the table. One of the guys watching his movements asked, "You want to play a game?"

Cisero replied, "Sure, why not." The guy racked the balls. Sensing Cisero was a novice to the game, he told him to break (shoot) first. Cisero proceeded to strike the cue ball, which hit the other balls, but not enough for any of them to drop into the pocket holes. Grabbing the other men's attention, they commenced the teasing of Cisero. One man said, "This is a big boy's game! The children's table is down the block at the day care!" as their friend began clearing the table with every strike he made with the balls. Every time the friend hit the ball into the pocket, they would cheer while simultaneously teasing Cisero. When he finally missed a shot, Cisero walked up to the table and made a few shots. When Cisero missed again, the guys, heartless as ever, laughed louder and harder while taunting him. By this time, a crowd began to form around the table to watch the game. The guy, with his final opportunity, cleared the table and won the game. Cisero became the pool table punching bag, because everyone wanted a chance to play and demolish him. Cisero, feeling hurt and taking advantage of, promised himself never to allow someone the chance to humiliate him on a pool table again. When Cisero got home, he was too upset to eat. He took a shower and went to bed.

The next day, Cisero went downstairs to visit Janie. Cisero told her every last detail of the evening. Janie could see Cisero was getting miffed as he relived what transpired. In a calm voice, Janie encouraged him to learn the game and then get his revenge rematch against those misfits. Cisero, absorbing what Janie expressed, became fully determined to improve his game. Cisero practiced at *John's Pool Room* on Fulton Street in Brooklyn, NY. Cisero studied the game every day, watching others play, and picked up some pointers to go with his own unique style. It wasn't long before the elder pool players started to notice and pay full attention to Cisero. Cisero felt it was time to find out how well his game had developed. He played players of all ages and delivered them tremendous defeats. Cisero played and practiced in various locations within New York City; one establishment was named *McCardies Pool Room*, located on Nostrand Ave in Brooklyn, NY. After having another conversation with Janie, they both concurred that it was time to have the long awaited rematch with the guys from the PAL. Cisero knew that the guys he wanted to play pool against would come during the evening time. Ideally, it was perfect, in his eyes, because the PAL would have enough witnesses to observe the thrashing he intended to inflict. Cisero strategically waited until Friday evening to go to the PAL. Once inside, he immediately proceeded to the second floor where the pool tables were located.

As he predicted, the same guys were already at the table. One of the men had started a game against another player. Holding to their routine, they were laughing and teasing the players competing against their friend. Cisero, without saying a word, just walked over to one of the empty pool tables and picked up a stick. Simultaneously, one of guys recognized him and stated, "Look who's back! Do you want another beating?"

The moment Cisero was waiting on had arrived; he knew their loud outbursts would draw a crowd. Cisero replied, "Sure, why not!" with a slight grin on his face. The guy who issued the challenge told Cisero to go first, and he complied. Unfortunately for him, Cisero's opening break was much different from the last time he played. Cisero didn't give the guy a chance to shoot, because he cleared all of his balls. The guy couldn't believe what had just happened. He immediately yelled, "That was luck!" Cisero just smiled. The crowd was going crazy with excitement. Cisero, being a good sport, returned the favor by letting the loser break first. The guy walked up to the table, took aim, and broke the rack of balls. One ball fell into the pocket, and the guy resumed his typical shenanigan behavior, which led to a full onset of laughter. The guy ran five balls off the table until he missed. Cisero got up from the chair, looked at the table for thirty seconds, and ran every single ball off the table. The crowd started cheering for Cisero, and the guy did not appreciate it. His other two friends didn't like what transpired either, and both of them challenged Cisero. Cisero accepted the challenges and obliterated the men. Cisero was very proud of himself that particular evening. Janie was also proud of him because he'd worked so hard to procure this goal. As a result of this moment, Cisero decided he was going to cease the boxing pursuit and become a professional pool player.

Chapter 9

The Legacy Begins

He continued his day time job as an auto mechanic, and at night he would practice on his pool game. One night, while practicing at the PAL, Cisero met another young pool player named James "Cornbread" Thomas. The two became great friends. At times, Cisero would practice with Cornbread. He admitted that Cornbread had a decent pool game. They both would hang out at every opportunity possible, to the point where if you saw one, the other was in close proximity. One weekend, Cisero was standing outside his residence conversing with Janie while waiting for Cornbread to arrive. As the two talked, Cornbread finally arrived at the house. Cisero introduced Janie to Cornbread, and they both greeted each other before Janie went inside the house. Cisero and Cornbread started walking to the PAL. Cornbread inquisitively asked, "Who was that fine lady you were talking to?"

Cisero replied, "My good friend!"

Cornbread further emphasized, "Shit, the way you were looking at her and the way you were acting, I thought she was your woman!"

James "Cornbread" Thomas

Cisero neither confirmed nor deny Cornbread's comments; he just smiled and simply changed the subject. Cornbread caught the hint and dropped the topic. Once they reached the PAL, both men went upstairs and practiced their game. As soon as people saw Cisero, they would gather around the table to watch. As he was practicing, Cisero overheard one of the spectators say, "Damn, he is good! I wonder if he's going to play in the upcoming pool event." Cisero wasn't aware of any PAL-sponsored pool tournament. Upon finishing practice, Cisero went to the PAL office to inquire about a possible pool event. The PAL staffed confirmed that there was going to be an event, and asked if he cared to partake. Undoubtedly, Cisero concurred and registered for the impending event.

A few weeks later, Cisero competed against some of the top pool players within the city of New York. He won the *New York City Championship* while in his teenage years. His family, Janie (his #1 fan), and the members of the community were proud of his accomplishment. Cisero, only in his teens, was considered to be one of the top competitors in the sport of billiards. Cornbread was equally proud, because he witnessed his practicing hard, and it paid off. Once the photo session and celebration were over,

Cisero bid everyone a good night. As he was departing, someone yelled out, "Good night, Champ!" This brought a smile to Cisero's face. When Cisero finally got home, he was exhausted. He took a shower and went straight to bed. The following morning, Cisero got to work early and started working on some cars. A few hours later, Cisero was called to the office. He thought his boss was going to congratulate him for winning the Championship; instead, Cisero was told he was being laid off due to lack of business. Cisero became disappointed, because he utilized the income to help his mother support the family. Later that evening, Cisero held a family meeting to inform everyone that he was now unemployed. He assured his mother that he would find another job soon and get back to helping the family. After the meeting, Cisero went back to his room (which he shared with James). Moments later, James walked in and saw Cisero resting on the bed. James assured Cisero that everything would work out. James then persuaded Cisero to hangout with him since he had some free time. Cisero admired his brother James because he dressed nice, had a lot of female friends, and was well-known in the streets. Cisero often refused because James would try to match him with one of his female friends, and the only female he was interested in was Janie. Cisero had to build up the courage to ask Janie to officially be his girlfriend. Cisero did allow James to show him where to go to buy clothes and shoes.

One weekend, Cisero and Cornbread was on their way to *John's Pool Room* because they heard out-of-towners were there playing pool, and they liked placing bets. Cisero, unemployed, saw this as a perfect opportunity to make a few dollars and test his skills in a different atmosphere. At the end of the night, Cisero walked away with a couple thousand dollars. Cisero shared some of the winnings with Cornbread. Cisero asserted, "This has got to be the easiest money I have ever made!"

Cornbread concurred and stated, "We should visit other pool rooms and take all bets!" They both walked down the long flight of stairs to the street level. Once they emerged onto Fulton Street, someone thought Cisero was his brother James. Cisero and James looked alike, and most often people mistakenly confused the two. Cisero at first would correct them, but, as the mishap continued, he would just listen to them and relate the message to James upon seeing him. Occasionally, he would let the individual(s) know where they could most likely find James, as he was known to be at the *Baby Grand Night Club*. Cisero and Cornbread proceeded to walk down Fulton Street toward *Kings Bar* on the corner of Marcy Avenue to pick up Cornbread's lady. The moment they reached Cornbread's lady, Cisero bid a good night and walked across the street to his residence.

Chapter 10

The First Family

The next day, Cornbread convinced Cisero that he could make more money traveling out of state playing pool. And so, Cisero and Cornbread would travel for weeks or months playing for money and winning. Cisero traveled and played so much that he didn't realize the distance he created between himself and Janie. Many months elapsed since Cisero and Janie last made contact. When Cisero came home, between road trips with Cornbread, he failed to reach out to Janie. This made Janie believe he wasn't interested in her. After waiting over a year, Janie met another guy. They dated for a while before she eventually got pregnant. She gave birth to a baby girl in February 1956. When Cisero learned that Janie met someone else and had a child, he was emotionally hurt. Cornbread immediately noticed Cisero's sudden change in behavior. This was the first time he'd seen him unstable. He asked Cisero, "What happened? What got you so uptight?" Cisero elaborated what had transpired. He confided in Cornbread his failure to let Janie know his true feelings, and that the lack of communication with her gave another man the opportunity to establish a bond. He further asserted, "I can't be mad at her, Cornbread; it was my stupid and selfish actions that caused this circumstance!"

Cornbread, looking Cisero straight in the eyes, pointed out, "I have never known you to give up; I know you to be a fighter!"

A few days later while Janie was leaving the medical office located at 237 Hancock Street from getting the youngster her vaccination shot, Cisero ran into her and asked if they could talk. Janie agreed to have a conversation with him later in the day. As the evening came, they met each other in front of their building and then walked to the public park on the corner of Macon Street and Tompkins Avenue. Once in private, Cisero began the conversation by telling Janie how he truly felt about her and how he regretted not informing her sooner. Janie, with tears in her eyes, interrupted him and expressed, "When you went on all those long road trips without saying a word to me, or, at least making one phone call to me, you made me think you didn't want to have anything to do with me!"

Janie further related that she felt alone and vulnerable. She elaborated that when she met her daughter's father, one thing led to another, and she became pregnant. Moreover, the two of them were no longer together, mainly because he didn't want to settle down, and her mom didn't approve of him. Cisero, reaching for her hand, related that he didn't fault her for living her life, that they couldn't change the past, and that they could only learn from their mistakes. He wanted her to know he loved her, and if she agreed to be his woman, he would stop going on road trips and find a local job. Janie immediately concurred, both happy and surprised. The surprising fact was that she thought he wanted nothing to do with her since she had a baby.

Janie Kearse and Cisero Murphy

Being a man of his word, Cisero found a job working as a laborer within a factory. During the evening hours, he would meet Cornbread, and together they would travel to the local pool rooms throughout New York City playing pool for money. As the months past, Janie and Cisero became inseparable. They spent a lot of quality time, and had frequent discussions about marriage. One evening, Cisero and Cornbread were playing pool at *John's Pool Room* when James came pushing past everyone until he found his younger brother. James pulled Cisero to the side and related that Janie was just taken to the hospital by the ambulance. Cisero, James, and Cornbread dashed out of the establishment onto Fulton Street. They hailed a cab, with the destination being *Kings County Hospital*. Upon arrival to the Emergency Room, Cisero met Sylvia (Janie's mom) there and asked, "How is she? What happened?" Sylvia related that Janie was complaining about feeling dizzy, and she was instructed to sit down and relax. A few moments later, there was a loud thump, and Janie was on the floor unconscious. Sylvia said she instantaneously called for help. Cisero sat beside Sylvia as they waited for the doctor to give updated information regarding Janie. About thirty minutes later, the doctor came over to address Cisero and Sylvia. The physician related that Janie had a mild concussion and would be held in the hospital for observation. The next morning, the doctor related that her tests were negative for any traumatic brain injury. He further stated that the likely source of Janie's dizziness was her pregnancy. The doctor cleared her to be discharged. Once leaving the hospital, all three of them were elated about Janie's impending baby. Upon arriving home, Cisero ran inside the building and upstairs, yelling for his mother. Eva, under the fallacy, after hearing him yelling, that he was in some trouble, grabbed her cast iron pan and opened her door to assist her son. Eva, seeing no one chasing him, said to Cisero, "Boy, what is wrong with you, making all this noise in the hallway?"

Cisero replied, "Janie is pregnant with my baby; I'm going to be a Dad!" Eva, having always liked Janie, was very blissful to know that Janie would be carrying her grandchild. Eva smacked Cisero in the back of the head. Cisero asked, "What is that for?"

Eva replied, "For making me think you were in trouble!" Cisero, looking down at his mother's hand, which was holding the pan, busted out into laughter.

Subsequently, Cisero further realized that his heart belonged to Janie. Cisero wanted to ensure that the entire day was considered completely perfect for Janie, him, and both families. He went to Janie's house to prepare a surprise dinner. Cisero, always having the ability but rarely performing it due to it being a female task, cooked a beautiful meal for both families to partake in. At the end of dessert, and everyone enjoying the evening, Cisero, doing what he wanted to do since their conversation in the park, grabbed Janie's hand and asked her to do him the honor of being his wife. Janie, entirely flabbergasted at the moment, with tears in her eyes ecstatically concurred to be Cisero's wife.

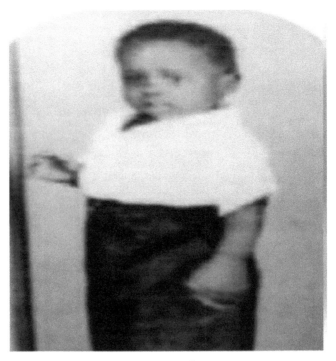

Cisero K. Murphy, Jr.

Months later, in November of 1957, Janie and Cisero became the proud parents of a baby boy. They named him Cisero K. Murphy, Jr. A few days later, Cisero Sr. walked through the doors of *Kings County Hospital* a gratified man because he came to pick up his woman and their son. All the family members were eager to meet the new addition. Once the cab pulled in front of 1342 Fulton Street, Janie's oldest sister, Nancy, was already downstairs waiting to lend a helping hand. Nancy carried Cisero Jr., because Janie felt a little weak, as Cisero Sr. carried the bags. As soon as they reached Cisero Sr.'s apartment, there was a welcome home banner on the front door. Upon opening the door, Janie was greeted by her and Cisero Sr.'s family members. Nancy carefully placed Cisero Jr. in the crib as everyone gathered around admiring and congratulating them both.

By the third week of January 1958, Cisero Sr. found an apartment for the family across the street, located at 22 Verona Place in Brooklyn, NY. Cisero Sr., Janie, Brenda, and Cisero Jr. settled into the new apartment quite comfortably. One evening, Cornbread came over to the house to see Cisero Jr. and to pick up Cisero Sr. so they could practice for the upcoming *New York State Championship*. Janie had no concerns with Cisero Sr. preparing for impending tournaments. However, she did have a problem with him being flirtatious with other females. Janie also expressed her discontent to Cisero Sr. about finding women's telephone numbers in his clothes during the course of her doing laundry. Cisero Sr. assured Janie that those numbers meant absolutely nothing to him and were just the numbers of fans he had no intent on contacting. He took a step closer to Janie, looked her in the eyes, and said that she was the only woman he loved and planned on marrying in the future. He gently gave her a kiss on the lips, opened the bedroom door, and walked into the living room where Cornbread was waiting; moments later, the two left. As they walked to the pool room, Cornbread asked, "What was the private meeting about; did I do or say something to upset her?"

Cisero laughed then replied, "No, she was upset because she found some female numbers in my pockets." Cornbread responded, "Wow, if that was my lady, I would be in the emergency room, right now!" They looked at each other and simultaneously burst into laughter as they began to jog up the stairs of *John's Pool Room.*

When they finished practicing, both men went across the street to the *Baby Grand Night Club.* As soon as Cornbread entered, he started mingling and socializing; meanwhile, Cisero walked over to the area where James was sitting with friends. Cisero joined them for a couple of hours before departing. By the time Cisero got home, Janie and the kids were already in bed. He walked into the children's room and kissed them both on the head. He took a shower, then went into Janie's and his room, gave her a kiss, and lay beside her, falling asleep himself. The next morning, Cisero awoke to the smell of bacon and eggs. He immediately washed up and joined the rest of the family at the breakfast table. Janie immediately noticed that Cisero was looking and acting very excited. Comically, Janie emphasized, "I see someone must have had a good night of sleep!"

Cisero replied, "Yes, I am very excited. I'm going to Kingston Park this morning to join the Brooklyn A's baseball team, as the pitcher."

Janie was very happy for him. Every Saturday morning, Cisero would meet his team at the park for practice. Shortly thereafter, Cisero became one of the key players on the squad. Cisero's first game was against a local Manhattan team named the Clinton Lions. Their star player was a second baseman named Roy Garcia. Cisero's powerful and lightening arm strength led the team to numerous victories. Before Cisero knew it, he found himself with a very busy routine. Janie, although supportive of Cisero's decision to play baseball and pool, was concerned due to his increasing less quality time with the family. As a result, Janie decided to confront Cisero about this frequent change in their family dynamic. Cisero listened attentively and apologized for his unexpected schedule. He further asked if she would show patience as he ascertained the best career to support the family. Naturally, Janie concurred to wait, but cautioned him not to forget his family. Cisero thanked her and added that he would reduce his practicing during the evening time. Happy they were able to reach an agreement, both hugged and kissed passionately.

Two weeks left before the tournament, Cornbread and Cisero made every practice session count. On the day of the tournament, Cisero kissed the children and told Janie that this win was dedicated to her. He kissed her intimately and then dashed out the door to a waiting taxi. When the taxi pulled in front of the PAL, he saw Cornbread outside waiting for him. Once outside the car, they both rushed inside to complete the registration process for the tournament. After playing some of the most talented and skillful players within the State of New York, Cisero won the *1958 New York State*

Billiards Championship. The opponents and spectators were completely mesmerized by how Cisero dominated the competition with mere ease. However, after their amazement, they humbly bid congrats and took pictures with him.

Cisero Murphy examining his next shot

The word was spreading fast within the billiards community about a young Negro, by the name of Cisero Murphy, who was a force to be reckoned with. The next day, Cornbread called Cisero to ascertain his plans for the day. Cisero expressed that the day was devoted for family time. Cornbread stated, "I need you to meet me at *John's Pool Room*; something came up."

Cisero pointed out, "I have my son. I have to watch him for a little while. Can we meet later?"

Cornbread was so relentless about Cisero's attendance that he told him to bring Cisero Jr. along; that the matter would only take a few minutes. Cisero concurred and then began to get Cisero Jr. and himself prepared for the trip. Twenty minutes later, unbeknownst to Cisero, Cornbread, in conjunction with James, had secretly planned a victory celebration. Cornbread held up his end by getting Cisero to come, and James was responsible for the selected guest invitations. Moments later, as promised, Cisero Sr. and Cisero Jr. arrived at *John's Pool Room*. When Cisero Sr. opened the door, both of them were greeted by fans. They opened bottles of champagne, engaged in small talk, and took pictures with the champ. However, Cisero Sr. decided to take a few pictures with Cisero Jr. by the pool table. In one picture, Cisero Sr. placed the pool stick in Cisero Jr. hands to make it appear like the youngster was holding it himself. James was elated to take the photos of his brother and nephew. James was eager to take the photo film to get developed at Pope's Photo Shop, and he ensured to have them the next day. Appreciating the urgency by his brother, Cisero Sr. gave acknowledgment. Cisero extended a graceful thanks for the celebration gathering, and proceeded to depart with Cisero Jr. in hand. As the two were about to exit the door, Cornbread and James told Cisero that they were having a small celebration to honor him at the *Baby Grand Night Club*. Cisero Sr. acknowledged and assured them that he would be in attendance later that night. Wittily, James told Cisero Sr. to take his nephew home; that he looked fatigued. All three of them shared the laugh, and then Cisero Sr. departed.

As soon as Cisero Sr. and Cisero Jr. walked through the door of the apartment, they were greeted by Janie. She gave Cisero Sr. a kiss and took Cisero Jr. out of his arms. Cisero told Janie where the two of them came from and what transpired. She wasn't upset; more along the lines of surprised. She didn't want young Cisero within that type of environment. Janie initially thought the two took a trip to visit the grandparents. Cisero, without missing a beat, assured Janie that he would never take Cisero Jr. there again. Cisero told Janie about the party for him later in the evening and asked if she would attend. Janie declined due to her not feeling well. Cisero asked if he should be worried, to which Janie told him she just needed a good night of sleep. Cisero then went to take a shower.

After the shower, Janie asked Cisero what he planned to wear to the function. Cisero was considering wearing something casual. Janie, in disagreement, instructed him to wear something formal. Pondering for a moment, Cisero came to his senses and realized that Janie was right. He pulled out a brown double-breasted suit with a beige shirt and corresponding accessories. When Cisero finished getting dressed, Janie looked at her fiancé and asked Cisero his question from earlier. "Should I be Worried?" They both burst into laughter. Janie complimented Cisero and gave him an intimate kiss before he walked out the door.

Cisero arrived at the *Baby Grand Night Club* around 10 p.m. As he walked inside, James met him at the door and immediately ushered him to the V.I.P section. As they made their way to the section, Cisero was impeded by many fans wanting to talk, take a picture, or his get an autograph. When they actually reached the table, there were people already seated. James introduced everyone to Cisero as they took their seats. Cisero noticed that there was an empty seat next to him, and he asked his brother if someone was seated there. James, with a smile, confirmed his question by saying, "Yes, little brother!" Moments later, Cisero noticed a fine woman approaching their table. As she got closer, all of the men stood up to greet her. James introduced her to everyone else normally, but when it came to Cisero, he gave it an extra flare. As James described, "Belinda, this is my brother Cisero, the Billiards Champion!"

Belinda, giving him a kiss on the cheek, stating, "I've heard so much about you. It's pleasure to finally get to meet you!"

Being polite, Cisero said, "The pleasure is mine!" as he held her chair while she simultaneously sat down. James decided to order more champagne for the table. He insisted that the disc jockey play some upbeat music to liven the place. Moments later, with everyone drinking and talking, the music began to sound good to Belinda and a few others. Belinda made the decision to ask Cisero to dance, which he accepted. Despite his dancing skills, Cisero did his best to keep with Belinda's pace. The more he kept pace, the more she danced sensually, drawing a crowd. The guys were cheering for Cisero, and the females were chanting Belinda's name. When the dance was over, the crowd applauded them both. Taking a break, Cisero and Belinda went back to the table. However, it was for a short moment, as the disc jockey played slow-paced music. Ready for round two, Belinda grabbed Cisero hand, leading him to the dance floor without one word being spoken. Once in the middle of the dance floor, she placed her arms around his neck, and with hers lips kissed his while simultaneously grinding against his body. Completely shocked, Cisero didn't do anything to stop Belinda. Moreover, so was Nancy, who was on the dance floor, unseen by Cisero. Once the song stopped, they all returned to their seats. Cisero wasn't sure if he should thank Belinda for the dance or act like it never transpired. Before he could finish his thoughts, Belinda had slid him a piece a paper with her phone number. Cisero accepted the paper, stood up, and announced he was going to leave. Cisero bid everyone a good night and walked toward the exit. While walking through the lounge area, he saw Nancy for the first time that evening sitting with friends. He walked over to her table and greeted everyone before he departed the establishment. Upon exiting and walking a short distance away, Cisero did three immediate things:

- First, he threw Belinda's phone number in the trash can to ensure Janie didn't have anything to worry about.
- Second, he aggressively wondered if Nancy witnessed any of the actions between Belinda and him, from the kiss to the seductive dance.
- He promised himself never to dance at any night club.

Moments later, Cisero arrived at the house and entered. Janie and the children were already sleeping. He got undressed and took a shower. Cisero kissed Janie's forehead, turned off the lamp, and went to sleep.

Chapter 11

The Point of No Return

The next morning, Cisero awoke early to make it to baseball practice. Janie awoke early with the intent to make Cisero's breakfast. Cisero thanked her, ate his food, grabbed his equipment, and then left for practice at the park. Subsequently, Janie made breakfast for the children when they awoke. Once the children finished eating, they all went to the living room to watch TV. As the children were occupied, Janie decided to do laundry. She started with the children's clothes and progressed to Cisero's clothing. As she separated Cisero's clothes, grabbing the items he wore from the previous night, she noticed what seemed to be a smudge of female makeup on his shirt. Carefully examining the shirt, Janie ascertained that it was female cosmetics. Janie became emotional, due to finding female numbers and now a makeup stain, every time she washed Cisero's laundry. When Cisero returned from baseball practice, he was greeted at the door by Janie. She, in a firm voice, let him know that they needed to converse. Curiously, Cisero wanted to know what the topic pertained to. While holding up the shirt, Janie ascertained, "About this! Are you cheating on me?"

Cisero was undoubtedly shocked. He had no idea that Belinda's makeup had smeared onto his shirt. Nevertheless, to answer Janie's question, Cisero stated, "No, I am not cheating on you!"

However, to Janie, his non-verbal communication was suggesting something else. Janie, unable to control her emotions, began crying while asking Cisero, "Whose makeup is this on your shirt?" As Cisero was about to answer, the phone rang. Janie attempted to ignore the phone, but the ringing wouldn't stop. Janie decided to answer the phone; it was Nancy. She told Nancy she couldn't talk because she was having an essential conversation. Not to be rejected, Nancy argued, "No! You need to hear what I have to say. It's about Cisero and what happened last night at the Baby Grand!"

Naturally, Janie wanted to hear what her sister was going to depict. Janie gave Nancy the permission to proceed. Nancy, in great detail, elaborated on how she'd seen a lady hug, kiss on the lips, and dance very seductively with Cisero. Meanwhile, Cisero stood silent during this entire process. He proceeded to walk around Janie, and she immediately informed him that they were not finished discussing this matter. He let her know he was going to the bathroom. Sarcastically, Janie said, "Why you have some more numbers to flush?" Cisero ignored the comment and went into the bathroom. Moments later, the conversation between the two sisters came to an end. Janie waited for Cisero to come out the bathroom before resuming the questioning. She asked, "So, who was the girl you were kissing on the dance floor?" Cisero, knowing Janie had a full depiction of what transpired, told Janie the truth about the previous night's events. He related that James introduced him to a variety of people, including a female named Belinda. Shortly after meeting, she asked him to dance, and he accepted. He further elaborated that once they got on the dance floor, unbeknownst to him, she placed her arms around him, kissed him, and then began to seductively dance on him. He concluded by saying that her conduct made him uncomfortable, and he left the club to come home. Janie, after assessing the confession, asked, "Did you know your brother was planning to introduce you to another female?"

Cisero replied, "No, I had no prior knowledge!" Janie began a harsh line of questioning towards Cisero to establish whether or not all individuals had malicious intent on depicting the disrespectful acts. Cisero reiterated to Janie that no one had mischievous objectives, and once he became uncomfortable, he instantaneously left. Janie, unfazed by Cisero's version of events, emphasized, "I will tell you what I do know. Since your brother

James has no respect for me, he is not welcome in my house. As for you, I think you should go live with your mother. I need some time to think about this relationship. I do not want to marry a cheater!"

She made it clear to Cisero that he needed time to seriously evaluate them and their relationship. Cisero, realizing he allowed this to happen, packed a few of his personal items and moved back in with his mother. Eva, surprised by Cisero's belongings, asked her son, "What is going on?" Cisero elaborated on what transpired, and she acted swiftly. Eva found James and emphasized, "You'd better do whatever it takes to make things right between your brother and Janie, or so help me!"

James made several attempts to reach out to Janie by phone and/or knocking on her house door. Janie ignored each and every attempt on purpose. Days later, James was walking down Herkimer Street and saw Janie with the children at the *Public School 93* playground. James's first intention was to walk past, but he remembered what Eva said and quickly headed toward Janie. Approaching Janie carefully, not to alarm her, James asked her if the two of them could talk. Janie immediately responded with a "NO!" James, being persistent, told Janie that his mother said he'd better make everything right. Janie said, "Okay, what do you have to say?"

James, in a sincere tone, apologized for deceiving Cisero and disrupting their lives. He further related that he led Cisero to believe that a sports writer from a magazine was going to interview him, and he had no knowledge of the blind date he'd setup for him. He also hid the plot from Cornbread. He concluded by saying that it was silly and begged for Janie's forgiveness. Janie said, "Okay!" Before departing, James told Janie that Cisero didn't know he was conducting this meeting, and that he wanted to keep it among them. James also related that Cisero may be in contact with her due to him being laid off from work and feeling depressed. Again, Janie said, "Okay!" James finally left and Janie went back to watching the children play. While the children played, Janie processed the information James gave her and realized that Cisero was truly a victim of James's nonsense. However, she wasn't going to take Cisero back so quickly, and she decided to let him continue to stay with his mother, hoping an imperative lesson would be learned.

Chapter 12

Three Strikes and You're Out!

Two weeks later, Janie allowed Cisero to return to the family. He told her about being laid off, and that the result of this action would give ample time with the family until he found other employment. Acting surprised, Janie related to him that she understood. Keeping to his word, Cisero, on his days off from looking for a job, would assist Janie with the family chores. Cisero and Cornbread still would meet to practice for the upcoming *Eastern State Championship Tournament* to be held at the PAL. Cisero and Cornbread decided to change the location where they trained. Cisero suggested *Amsterdam Billiards* located in Harlem, NY, due to the establishment having nice-sized tables and plenty of side gambling action. Cornbread smiled and told Cisero, "Now you're speaking my language!"

One day while Cisero was job searching, Janie received a call meant for Cisero. The caller was reaching out to offer Cisero a driver/delivery position. He related that if Cisero was interested, he needed to come to an interview with two forms of identification in the morning. Janie wrote all the information, including the time and location, on a piece of paper. Once the conversation was complete, both of them hung up the telephone. Hours later when Cisero returned home, Janie informed him about the employment opportunity. Eagerly, Cisero took the piece of paper from Janie while simultaneously thanking her. The next morning, Cisero followed the directions and reported to the location. After a thirty-minute interview, Cisero was hired for the position. On the way home, Cisero stopped to buy flowers for Janie. As he walked through the apartment door, Janie realized something good had transpired. Cisero confirmed Janie's notion when he gave her the flowers and revealed that he'd start work the following week. He further related that the employer paid weekly. Cisero and Janie, both ecstatic, shared multiple kisses before she returned to the kitchen to finish cooking dinner. The financial pressure Cisero felt came to ease since he had steady employment. Cornbread was pleased, because it meant his friend's persona would depict a relaxed and stress-free vibe, which was great to have in the world of billiards.

A few weeks later, Cisero signed up to participate in the *1959 Eastern State Championship Tournament.* The location was going to be on Gates Avenue in Brooklyn, New York. One night, Cornbread informed Cisero that he arranged a game against some guys from New Jersey. Cornbread wanted them to meet at the *Blue Ribbon Night Club,* located on Fulton Street in Brooklyn, NY, to discuss their game strategy. Cisero concurred, and the pair decided to meet at 7:30 p.m.

Later that evening, Cisero arrived on time to the preset location, but Cornbread was nowhere in sight. Cisero was frustrated with Cornbread's lateness, because he encountered slight discomfort being within those drinking atmospheres by himself. Cisero, while sitting down, noticed that the barmaid was giving him more attention than the other guests. Initially, he thought it was due to him being within the establishment for a period of time without ordering anything. However, she was eyeing him because she recognized exactly who Cisero was and she wanted to meet him before he departed. Moments later, Cornbread finally arrived at the night club. Cisero, very irritated, asserted, "I bet, you better be on time for our next meeting, or I will leave!"

Cornbread, while looking at Cisero, inquired, "How come you always say, "I bet" in everything you say?"

Cisero immediately dictated, "I bet you better sit your ass down!"

The two of them looked at each other and then began to laugh immensely. Before they could discuss their strategic plan, the same barmaid, named Sunshine, came over and said, "How are you doing, CB?"

Cornbread stood up and acknowledged her. Cisero followed by standing, and it gave Sunshine the opportunity to officially meet him. She immediately said, "Hello, Champ!" cutting off Cornbread's attempt to introduce them to each other. Sunshine, like a true fan, asked if they could take a picture together, and Cisero humbly agreed. After the photos were taken, Sunshine returned to the bar. As she walked away, Cisero couldn't help noticing her well-shaped body. Once at the bar, Sunshine looked back at Cisero, the two made eye contact, and she blew him a kiss, to which he nodded his head in appreciation. Cisero turned his attention back to Cornbread and the reason for their meeting. Once the meeting concluded, Cisero looked at Cornbread and informed him that he liked his nickname. Cisero said, "Talk to you later, CB!" to which Cornbread laughed.

For the next month, Cisero and CB practiced profusely. The day of the tournament was upon them, and Cisero appeared completely relaxed. Janie was determined to attend the event to support her fiancé. She called her younger sister, Christalee, to watch the children. Once Christalee arrived, Cisero grabbed his gear and they both left. They hailed a taxi on Fulton Street to the PAL on Gates Avenue. When Cisero and Janie reached the PAL, Cornbread was outside awaiting their arrival in order to help them into the establishment. Once inside, Cisero instantaneously walked over to the office to register into the tournament. Meanwhile, Cornbread escorted Janie to her sitting location for the duration of the event. Subsequently, Cisero joined them at the table. Cisero walked toward the officials once they began to make announcements while simultaneously shaking the hands of participants, some of whom he knew. He proceed to the table assigned to him, looked in Janie's direction, blew her a kiss, and commenced the game.

After playing some great diverse opponents, Cisero defeated each adversary with tremendous ease to capture the *1959 Eastern State Championship*. Janie and his supporters were out of control with excitement. Enthusiasts waited patiently, in a line, to congratulate and take a picture. However, Janie asserted her presence with Cisero to let the flirtatious female fans be aware that she would not tolerate their behavior. Cisero ended the session, gently grabbed Janie's hand, and proceeded to the exit. Once outside, Cornbread signaled them to come over to where he had a taxi awaiting. Before Cisero stepped inside the taxi, a few guys greeted him and inquired if they could set up a couple of private games for money. Cisero informed them that he was fatigued and heading home with his fiancée, and that they could discuss the details with Cornbread. The men acknowledged, and shortly after, the taxi departed.

Cisero Murphy while taking final aim

As Cisero and Janie reached home, she quickly kicked off her shoes and collapsed onto the living room couch. Cisero walked toward Christalee and paid her for watching the children. Upon Christalee's departure, Janie and Cisero opened a bottle of Champagne to celebrate privately. The following morning, Cisero awoke early because he had baseball practice to attend. When he returned home, he took a shower and joined the family in the living room watching television. Later in the evening, Cisero decided to go out for a couple of hours. He got dressed, kissed Janie and the children, and then exited the apartment. As he reached outside, Cisero ran into Cornbread. After a few moments of conversing, the two concurred to go play a few games for money. Cisero's night life was going great; he won more games for money, and the result of this was him spending less time in the home. Janie started hearing rumors of Cisero and a caramel-complexioned female. She didn't mention anything to Cisero because she didn't have proof and didn't want to appear paranoid. However, it was clear to Janie that Cisero's attitude towards her seemed to be changing.

One weekend, Janie awoke the same time as Cisero. As he got ready for baseball practice, she got all the dirty clothes together to go to the laundry. Before leaving, he asked if she needed help, but she declined, because Christalee was coming over. Typically they would go together, but Cisero Jr. wasn't feeling well. Cisero acknowledged her and then departed to practice at *Kingston Park*. An hour later, Janie decided to try the new laundromat on the corner of Nostrand Avenue and Macon Street. Janie walked inside the establishment and realized it didn't have large machines, and the cost was too expensive. Janie chose to go to the other facility on Macon Street and Marcy Avenue, just down the block. Upon the first load of clothes being washed and placed in the dryer, Janie returned home to get a second load. Once back at the laundry, she realized there wasn't enough detergent, and walked to the supermarket. As she journeyed toward the market, Janie instantly became upset because she couldn't believe what her eyes depicted. Janie witnessed Cisero and the caramel-complexioned female hugging each other on the corner of MacDonough Street. As they were about to kiss, Janie interrupted them with a thunderous and vicious yell of "CISERO!" Cisero was startled and embarrassed. As he turned toward the direction of Janie's voice, he only got a quick glance of her before he felt her sprint past and begin attacking the female. Janie had the female on the ground, throwing massive connecting blows to her face. Finally able to grab her, Cisero pulled Janie off the girl. Janie, in an enraged tone, asserted, "GET YOUR HANDS OFF ME; DO NOT TOUCH ME!! You have cheated on me for the last time. WE ARE THROUGH!"

Janie walked back to the laundry, took the dirty clothes out of the machine, and then went home. Christalee saw that Janie was extremely upset, and inquired. Janie related to her what had transpired, and her reaction, which totally shocked Christalee. Janie requested her to retrieve the remaining clothes from the laundromat, to which Christalee agreed. Upon Christalee's return to the house, Janie asked if she would stay the night, because she didn't want to be alone.

A few days later, Janie allowed Cisero inside the apartment to pack all his possessions. Although their relationship was completely finished, they concurred to be loving and supportive parents of their son, Cisero Jr. Cisero and his brothers made multiple trips to relocate his personal property to his mother's house. Two weeks later, Janie found an apartment located at 1360 Fulton Street. She secured a part-time job at a local dry cleaning shop on the same street. The first few months were difficult for Janie and the children, especially during the holidays. Janie admitted that she still loved Cisero, due to their history. The breakup was necessary, however painful, because of his appetite for other women.

Chapter 13

We Shall Overcome and Prevail in the Face of Hate

After the physical altercation amongst Janie and the caramel-complex-ioned girlfriend, Cisero vowed to never allow them to cross paths. In 1960, Cisero's game of straight pool was unbeatable. For the second time, he went on to capture the *Eastern State Championship*. Cornbread and Cisero couldn't wait to travel the road. On the weekends, they traveled throughout New York to play for money. One evening in December of 1960, moments before the next game started, Cisero decided to call home. A few minutes into the conversation, Cisero's mother inquired whether or not he'd spoken to his lady friend, because she was anxious to speak to him. Cisero informed his mother that he didn't have a dialog with his friend. The game was ready to start. Cisero related to his mother that he'd reach out to her on his next break, told her goodbye, and then hung up. Cornbread probed Cisero to ensure things were good. Cisero confirmed that matters were well. As they walked toward their opponents, Cornbread said, "Great, now let's get this money!" to which both men laughed.

Twenty minutes later, the guy missed his shot, and Cisero never gave him another chance as he ran all of his balls off the table. When the game was over, Cisero started breaking down his pool stick while Cornbread handled the finances. Since he had five minutes, Cisero decided to call his girlfriend. Shortly into their conversation, Cisero became very excited, and it was very noticeable to everybody else. Cisero proudly announced that he was going to be a father for the second time. Cornbread, equally elated, questioned what the next move would be, to which Cisero dictated, "I bet you'd better go get the damn car and take me home!"

Cisero Murphy's famous hesitation Stroke from the corner

Cornbread acknowledged the command and then led the way toward the exit. As Cisero neared the exit, a few guys yelled out supportive cheers, which he recognized by saying, "Thanks!"

On the way back to New York City (NYC), Cisero and Cornbread concurred to suspend all road trips until after the holidays. Subsequently, Cisero signed up to compete in the *1961 Pool Tournament* at the PAL. The year 1961 was extraordinary for Cisero. He won the *Eastern State Cham-*

pionship for the third consecutive year. Lastly, in August 1961, his girl-friend gave birth to his second child, a baby girl.

Cisero Murphy poses for the camera

In 1962, Cisero's billiards game was invincible, and the direct result led to a fourth year straight as *Eastern State Championship Winner*. Unconquerable, one of many single-word depictions, was the word Cisero's fans utilized to describe his pool game after witnessing him win the *1963 Eastern State Championship* for the fifth time. In that year, Cisero Jr. began his first year in elementary education at *Public School 93*.

Cisero Murphy displays his famous hesitation stroke.

In 1964, despite incredible personal attributes, Cisero endured a dramatic obstacle. Cisero was a black man dominating a sport which was considered to be a "Whites only" sport during the *Jim Crow Laws* within the United States. Cisero wasn't invited to play in many competitions, including, but most essentially, the *1964 World Title Tournament*, despite his recognized talent and professional winning record. In an attempt to justify the discriminatory act against Cisero, officials related that he didn't play enough, and that his name wasn't a "familiar name" in the sport. When the news of Cisero's rejection to compete in the *'64 World Tournament* was made public, a variety of players, including Caucasians and supportive fans, boycotted outside the *Commodore Hotel* in Burbank, California. Protesters demanded that they let Cisero play in the title event. Instead of inviting Cisero to play in the competition, he was told he had to enter and win more games before he could qualify for the title tournament. Let us be perfectly clear—Cisero was a victim of discrimination solely because of his skin. However, he didn't let their negativity deter him. Cisero was determined to prove to the billiards community that he was a force to be reckoned with.

Cisero Murphy after a successful tournament

Many of those who played against Cisero in the *Eastern State Tournament*, as well as the spectators, all agreed that Cisero's game was incapable of being surmounted. Accordingly, Cisero won the *1964 Eastern State Championship*, making it the sixth year straight. Cisero signed up and participated in the *1964 New York City Championship Tournament*. He successfully won the tournament for the second time in his professional career. A few weeks later, Cisero entered and successfully won the *1964 State Summer League Tournament*. Upon winning this tournament, Cisero automatically became eligible to compete in the *1965 World Invitational Tournament*. Cisero credited many professional pool players and his supporting fans, who marched on the picket line in protest, as a contributing facet to his being invited to play in the world title.

Chapter 14

The Second Family

In August 1964, Cisero accumulated enough finances to purchase a house located at 77 Hancock Street, in the Bedford Stuyvesant section of Brooklyn, NY. Cisero moved his mother and other family from 1342 Fulton Street to the new house. A few weeks later, he moved his girlfriend and all of her children to Hancock Street. The girlfriend, outside of her and Cisero's child, already had three children, aged sixteen, fourteen, and twelve, from three different men along the east coast.

On Thursday, October 15, 1964, Cisero and his girlfriend got married in the living room of the new house. Although this was Cisero's first marriage, the same could not be said for his new wife, as this was her second attempt at marriage. Cisero was even more elated whenever he wasn't traveling, because he would sit in his favorite chair, polish his pool sticks, and simultaneously watch his preferred TV shows. He could never get enough viewings of *I Love Lucy, My three Sons, Hazel*, and/or *Happy Days*. One evening, Cisero's wife entered their bedroom to check on him, because she noticed he wasn't acting his usual self. She asked, "What's wrong? Do you want to talk about it?" Cisero looked at his wife and confided to her how he was upset about not being invited to play in the *1964 World's Title Tournament* simply because he was black. She walked over to Cisero, sat on the arm of the chair, reached over to hug him, and in a soft, consoling voice, emphasized, "No man can stop God's plan! You are a remarkable man representing the black race during a time of racial discrimination. Stay focused on your grandfather's prophecy for strength. When you play in next year's title competition, walk in there with the total mindset of a champion, and you will be victorious!

She got up and walked toward the dining room, where the rest of the family was seated. Waiting for the head of the house to take his place at the table, Cisero's wife stopped suddenly, turned back in his direction, and, using one of his lines, expressed, "I bet, you better get yourself over to the dinner table as soon as possible; the children are getting impatient!"

Cisero looked at her, smiled, then replied, "I will be right there!"

Chapter 15

Who Is This Guy?? Murphy, Cisero Murphy

Cisero Murphy and George Balabushka, legendary cue designer

In 1965, Cisero Murphy broke racial barriers and set milestone records in the sport of billiards by becoming the first and only Black competitor to win all fourteen matches, in a row, to capture *The World Invitational 14.1 Tournament* on his first attempt. Murphy defeated Caucasian player Luther Lassiter in the final match. The billiards community, including Murphy, considered him to be the "Jackie Robinson" of billiards. Murphy's supporters believed in his skills. People from different walks of life all joined together to celebrate their champion's victory. Murphy's local community members were very proud of his accomplishments and displayed the affection at a parade, in his honor, during Brooklyn Day.

Cisero K. Murphy, Jr. during a class session

Many of the teachers from *Public School 93*, who educated Murphy when he was in elementary education, were gratified with him. A few educators who knew his son, Cisero Jr., attended the school and went to the third grade classroom to capitalize on the photo opportunity with their "Black hero" relative. In the PAL where Cisero first picked up a pool stick, a picture mural of him was painted on the 2nd floor wall in his honor. Another picture was located on the wall of a building on Washington Avenue and the corner Empire Boulevard, in the Flatbush section of Brooklyn, NY. Additionally, *Jet Magazine* wrote a segment regarding Murphy in their sports section in the March 25, 1965 printed issue, entitled *Negro Stick Wiz, Win Pocket Billiard Title.*

Cisero Murphy and a fellow billiards enthusiast

In 1966, Cisero's professional billiards record was becoming more impressive. He won, continuing his dominance, the *1966 Stardust Open Championship* in Las Vegas. Cisero competed in many billiard competitions, which were financially profitable. As a direct result, Murphy made the decision to stop working odd jobs to support his family. This resolution included professional softball, because his passion for billiards was too great. In an effort to build his professional brand, Cisero, along with a few other associates, made strides toward formulating a corporation and/or business ventures with no avail. However, Murphy was successful enhancing his brand through the media. Additionally within that year, Murphy was interviewed by Harry Reasoner of CBS News. Next, on Thursday, June 23, 1966, *Jet Magazine* wrote another article about Murphy entitled, *Cisero Murphy on Cue in Billiards Tournament.* Following suit, *Ebony Magazine* wrote an article pertaining to Murphy in their September publication, entitled *Pool Shark from Brooklyn.* In November, his wife gave birth to his third child, their second kid together, another baby girl.

On January 12, 1967, *Jet Magazine* wrote their third article on Murphy, in the *New York Beat* section, on page 64. In their fourth and final article covering Murphy, on March 16, 1967, *Jet Magazine* wrote a piece on page 42 in their *People Are* section. Furthermore, P. Paul Provost from *Ebony Legends in Sports Magazine* wrote an article entitled *Pool/ Billiards.* In addition, Calvin W. Maxwell Jr., from the *American Pool Player Magazine*, published a segment entitled *Make Every Shot Count*, depicting Murphy. Also in 1967, Murphy appeared on a radio talk show with Minnesota Fats in ST. Louis, Missouri, for a Q and A session.

Chapter 16

The Hustle and a Bond

In 1968, Cisero had the pleasure of meeting and playing pool with William "Red" Shoates. They played many games together and became good friends. Red was an excellent pool player, in his own right. Their games came to a brief cease when Red enlisted in the United States Military. For the next few years, Cisero would travel between major tournaments to various states such as Nevada, California, New Jersey, Missouri, Georgia, and Illinois to play games. One could say, especially Cisero, that he was very financially successful during his interstate travels.

William "Red" Shoates

In 1970, at the age of thirty-five, Murphy participated in the *World's Invitational Pocket Billiard Championship Tournament* held in Los Angeles, California. After the tournament, Murphy caught the first flight to New York. As soon as Cisero's plane landed at *John F. Kennedy International Airport,* formally known as *New York International*, Cornbread was there to transport him home. During the ride, Cornbread seized the opportunity to let Cisero know his girlfriend was pregnant. Cisero was elated for his best friend. They chitchatted in regards to the joy of fatherhood, and then switched the conversation to billiards. Cornbread immediately told Cisero about some high rollers he met at *John's Pool Room.* Cornbread further related the preliminary specifics; it would be twenty dollars a ball, with side bets. Cisero, liking what he heard, gave Cornbread the head-nod approval to make the necessary arrangements. The last thing Cisero heard before falling asleep was Cornbread acknowledging his confirmation. Forty-five minutes later, Cornbread pulled up in front of Cisero's house. Cisero exited the car, grabbed his bags from the backseat, thanked him for the ride, and congratulated him on the impending baby. Cornbread recognized his praise and replied, "You are welcome!" Cisero told his good friend they'd talk later. As he walked into the house, Cornbread simultaneously drove off.

Two days later, Cisero met Cornbread at *John's Pool Room*. After a brief discussion, Cornbread introduced Cisero to his opponent, a middle-aged man from Texas who went by the name Jake. Once both sides completed their financial discussion, the game began. A few hours later, Cisero won four out of the seven games. His total winnings were twenty-five hundred dollars in cash. Cornbread collected all the side-bet earnings. When the financial affairs were completed, all four men shook hands and went their separate ways. Once on the street level, Cisero decided to walk Cornbread to his car. Cornbread, excited about the win, told Cisero he knew of other locations where which they could get paid. Cisero just laughed. He loved to see how amused Cornbread would get, because it reminded him of a kid in a candy store. Not wanting to spoil his friend's mood, he concurred with Cornbread, setting up a few more games. A few months later, Cornbread's girlfriend gave birth to a beautiful baby girl. Cisero and a few other close associates put a cash envelope together and he delivered it to Cornbread's house. This also allowed Cisero to see the infant and to congratulate both parents.

Chapter 17

A Legend, a Teacher, and His Students

In 1973, Cisero's wife gave birth to his fourth and final biological child, a baby boy. Cornbread was exhilarated for his best friend. Once the news traveled of Cisero's new family addition, many of his friends assembled a monetary gift and entrusted Cornbread to make the delivery. After Cornbread delivered the envelopes, he sat with Cisero to reminisce about their childhood, from years they grew up without a father to their crazy teenage years. As fathers, they vowed to each other to be present during the growth and development of their children's lives. Cornbread further emphasized, "I guess this would be the right time to mention, I can't go with you on anymore long distance road trips. I'm planning to marry my lady, and I'll be starting a job to support my family. I can do some local trips once in awhile, particularly on weekends, but I have to be home with family come the end of each day."

Cisero looked at his best friend, and asserted, "I entirely understand the value of having a father present. To be honest, I was seriously planning to slow down myself. As for your request to accompany me on some local trips, sounds like an excellent idea!"

Cisero congratulated cornbread on his decision to get married. At the conclusion of their heartfelt conversation, Cornbread briefly embraced Cisero while simultaneously thanking him for being so supportive. Cisero told his best friend that he was welcome; then Cornbread departed.

Cisero Murphy during an exhibition

For the next few years, Cisero, with Cornbread's assistance, arranged to play in local pool halls throughout NYC. Cisero decided to utilize his God-given abilities to help enhance society. He successfully contributed to the *Pool in the Streets Program* initiated and sponsored by *The New York City Department of Parks and Recreation*. Cisero would gathered a few kids from the community to help set up the pool table. Using a van as transportation, he would travel throughout all five boroughs of NYC giving free trick-shot exhibitions. He visited various locations, such as Senior Citizen Homes, Veterans Hospitals, and Mental Health Facilities. Cisero procured great pleasure in his pedagogy of people regarding how to play pool and other imperative facets within the world of billiards.

David "Blackjack" Sapolis

In 1979, while playing a few games in *John's Pool Room*, Cisero noticed a boy being ushered out by one of the establishment's personnel. As they neared his table with the boy he'd seen inside on several occasions, Cisero shouted at the attendant, "Let the kid stay!" Upon hearing the command, the staff member released the youngster. Now free and full of excitement from not being exiled, the adolescent could watch the games. He journeyed over to the voice that saved him and gazed at Cisero playing, in amazement. When the game was over, Cisero approached the young boy and asked, "What's your name?" The boy looked at Cisero and replied, "My name is David Sapolis." Cisero began a serious of questions to ascertain whether or not David was authentic. David would respond to the questions, but Cisero knew the depiction was false and made him aware of the dubiousness. After getting to the truth, Cisero felt obligated to make sure David returned home safely. Leaving the pool room, Cisero placed David in his car and drove him to his residence in New Jersey. During the ride, Cisero found himself speaking in an authoritative nature toward David. Cisero wanted to reinforce that honesty and education were essential facets in life. Cisero concurred to educate David about billiards, providing he adhered to the strict guidelines set forth during their conversation. At first David didn't approve of the stipulations, but over time he appreciated the pedagogy and firm support from Murphy.

Chapter 18

New Ventures and a New Generation

In 1980, Cisero decided to diversify his night life activities. He began working as a manager in a new Brooklyn club for a long-time acquaintance. *The Arizona* was the newest and hottest night spot, located at 2575 Fulton Street in Brooklyn, NY. One evening, before operating hours, the owner wanted to introduce Cisero to her boyfriend. As soon as Cisero entered the office, they simultaneously stood up from behind her desk, to greet Cisero. She emphasized, "Cisero, I'd like you to meet my man, Joseph "Strokey" Armstrong."

Joseph "Strokey" Armstrong

Both men shook hands to signify acknowledgment of each other. For the next fifteen minutes, all three of them conversed until it was time to open for business. As time passed, Cisero and Strokey became good friends. One weekend while Cisero was practicing in a local pool room, he noticed Strokey enter the establishment carrying a pool stick case. As soon as Strokey reached close enough to the table, Cisero looked up and engaged his friend by asking, "How you doing, Strokey?"

Strokey pointed out, "I am fine, my brother! I just came out to shoot a couple of games. Do you want to play a few 'friendly' games?"

Cisero hesitated a moment, then replied, "Just a couple; I have some important errands to attend to."

Intrigued by the name, Cisero asked, "How did you get the name Strokey?"

In a joking manner, Strokey replied, "I'm about to show you!" in which both men laughed. When the game began, Cisero instantaneously observed his friend's interesting stroke when hitting the cue ball. Strokey's game was extraordinary, but no match for Cisero. When the contest was over, both men settled their financial business. Before departing, Cisero inquired if Strokey would be at the club later, and his friend confirmed he'd be in attendance.

Tyriek A. Murphy, Cisero's first grandchild

By 1982, life was going great for Cisero. Cisero's existence became more rewarding upon news from Cisero Jr. during a written communication notifying him of the new title he earned of grandfather. In February of 1982, Cisero was overwhelmingly ecstatic when he was able to meet and hold his first grandchild, named Tyriek A. Murphy. Cisero knew, during this moment within the hospital, that his grandson would accomplish a goal which had escaped a Murphy. Cisero, gazing at the handsome offspring, began a prognostication of Tyriek being the family's first college graduate. Minutes before leaving, he gave Tyriek a kiss on the forehead and returned him to the awaiting arms of Renee Humphrey, the youngster mother. As Cisero journeyed home, he repeatedly envisioned how exhilarating the day would be when his grandson fulfilled his prophecy. He simultaneously pondered if Cisero Jr. would ever cease his repeated illegal activities which resulted in various periods of incarceration. Cisero knew firsthand the emotional and mental effects that growing up without a father would render on a kid. Undoubtedly, he hoped Cisero Jr., upon release, would be a contributing facet to his grandchild's foreseen family greatness. In the years to follow, Cisero would have other grandchildren.

Cisero Murphy lining up a safety shot

As years passed by, Cisero would continue to practice and play pool games with, or without, some of his skilled friends. Although he didn't travel away frequently, as he did while in his prime, he still hustled a few games of pool or would participate in professional events. Despite Cisero retiring from competitive pool, he was well regarded as one of the top players in straight pool competitions. Murphy maintained his notion of helping individuals partake in and enjoy the sport of billiards, regardless of one's status.

Chapter 19

The Beginning to the End of a Legacy

One summer afternoon in 1994, Cisero decided to walk from his home to *John's Pool Room*. Along the way, he met a longtime friend, Lee "Big Lee" Bynum. Big Lee wasn't a pool shark; however, he could give the average player a good challenge.

As Cisero and Lee shook hands, he inquired as to how Lee and his family were doing. Lee retorted that everyone was in North Carolina and doing fine. As both men started walking toward Fulton Street, Lee questioned Cisero to find out his immediate agenda. Cisero informed him, and Lee revealed his knowledge about Cisero traveling to different spots and winning. While Cisero smiled from his comments, Lee then requested if he could finance some games the next time Cisero took any trips. Appreciating the gesture, Cisero elaborated to Lee he didn't travel much, but would keep the offer in mind. After exchanging contact information, Cisero and Lee went their separate ways.

As Cisero entered and started running up the stairs of *John's Pool Room*, he stopped halfway on the stairs due to an immensely incisive sensation within his chest. He disregarded the pain and didn't seek medical advice. When he finally made it to the top of the stairs, Cisero heard a familiar voice shout, "Man, you look terrible! Are you alright?" Cisero looked in the direction of the voice, and it was Cornbread.

Cisero pointed out, "Those damn stairs are going to kill somebody one day. I'll be okay; give me a few minutes!"

Moments later, Cisero stood straight up on his feet and walked over to his favorite table to practice. Three hours later, Cisero decided to go home to get rest, because he had to work at *the Arizona* that night. As always, Cisero arrived at the club early to make sure each area was properly staffed and ready for operations. For the next year, this would be Cisero's routine, including the ignoring of his increasing imperative health facet.

Over the decades, Murphy remained troubled with concept of not securing the recognition he gratefully earned. One can objectively insist that it was residual aspects of racial discrimination prohibiting his advancement. Murphy, along with his lifetime supporters, couldn't fathom how players he beat in professional competitions were graced with being inducted into the *Billiards Congress of America Hall of Fame* (BCA) over him. Multiple players during and after his professional career, particularly ones he paved the way for, were blessed with the opportunity. Murphy, remembering his snub from the *1964 World Title Tournament*, was deeply miffed, because the BCA officials ascertained that his contributions were inferior to those they selected. Murphy's well known, steadfast patience ultimately came to an end when the BCA officials declared him eligible for induction.

Billiard Congress of America Hall of Fame Banquet
A Tribute To

Cisero Murphy
July 29, 1995
Bally's Hotel & Casino
Las Vega, Nevada

The actual BCA Hall of Fame pamphlet

Accordingly, on Saturday, July 29, 1995, within the Bally Hotel and Casino, in Las Vegas, Nevada, Cisero Murphy was finally awarded the distinct honor of being inducted into the BCA. The ceremony brought out all the key pioneers of the sport and those inspiring to have their names solidified in BCA history.

David "Blackjack" Sapolis, Murphy's mentee

One of Murphy's key supporters was David Sapolis. Sapolis now as an adult enjoyed the concept of his mentor being presented with the one component which was missing from Murphy's illustrious career resume. By the end of all the BCA events, Cisero Murphy took his place as the only Black American to be both the world title winner and Hall of Fame inductee in the sport of billiards.

Cisero Murphy's BCA Hall of Fame ring

Cisero Murphy at BCA ceremony event

Cisero Murphy at BCA activity event

Cisero Murphy at BCA activity event

Cisero Murphy during a BCA event

Chapter 20

The Sun Don't Shine Forever

By April 1996, Cisero had accomplished most of his goals, and he continued to fulfill those left incomplete. He was undoubtedly a local inspiration. Despite all of his great attributes, one of Murphy's gravest fallacies was the lack of attention given to his medical health.

On April 20, 1996, like any other Saturday, Cisero got himself together and proceeded to take care of errands. Before departing the house, he gave Strokey a call on the phone. The two men agreed to meet at the racetrack. Cisero got a few items completed, including picking up his paycheck. Murphy encountered an acutely painful sensation, stronger than the symptom felt climbing those stairs at *John's Pool Room*, in his chest. While in the midst of crossing the intersection of Atlantic Avenue and Utica Avenue, Cisero endured a massive heart attack. The medical incident caused Cisero to instantaneously crash his car. By the time medical professionals reached Murphy, he was fatally wounded. When the news traveled of Murphy's death, everyone was either stunned or in total disbelief—no one more so than Strokey, mainly because he'd communicated with Cisero hours earlier and had immediate plans to gather socially.

This unforeseen, tragic event brought a big hurt to all of those affected by Murphy's inspirational pedagogy, whether friend or family. Murphy's funeral service was held in Brooklyn, NY. The ceremony brought plenty of people out to pay their final respects to an unsung icon. Of those hundreds of individuals, a few were high-profile members of the billiards world. Race was not a concern as both African and Caucasian Americans joined to bid Murphy a final farewell. Murphy was survived by his wife, children, grandchildren, and an abundance of other family and friends.

The Funeral Services
For

Cisero Murphy

October 2, 1935 - April 20, 1996

Funeral Services
Wednesday, April 24, 1996 - 7:00 P.M
Monks Memorial
1880 Fulton Street, Brooklyn, New York
Bishop Anthony Monk = Officiating

Interment - Thursday, April 25, 1996
Rosehill Cemetery
Linden, New Jersey

Arrangements For Mr. Cisero Murphy Were Entrusted To:
Lewis Funeral Services
162 4Th Avenue, Brooklyn, New York

Cisero Murphy's Necrology

Epilogue

Cisero S. Murphy was undoubtedly a bright light in American History, specifically Black American History. To achieve the attributes he accomplished, during the severity of racial tension within the United States, was unimaginable. Murphy's calm and focused demeanor led him to ultimately procure elite levels for the black population. Murphy self proclaimed himself, as well as others, to be the "Jackie Robinson" of the world of billiards. His ability to diversify this sport, predominately played by Caucasians, paved the way for others, including women, to partake.

Murphy, from his elementary to senior years, posted renowned records in the sport of billiards. Whether it was his sixth straight year *Eastern State Championship* run or his fourteen straight matches to acquire the covenant world title, Murphy's progressions have never been duplicated. As it stands currently within this twenty-first century, Cisero S. Murphy is the *only* Black American to win *The World Invitational 14.1 Tournament* on the first attempt and be inducted into the *Billiards Congress of America Hall Of Fame*. His fortitude has given many the inner strength to overcome the roadblocks once viewed as permanent obstacles.

Decades after his death, the pedagogy of Murphy has lived through those he affected. However, his identity has not reached the entire world, like other regularly discussed black pioneers, particularly athletes. Moreover, with the circulation of this literary piece, formal and informal educational sessions, and subsequent projects regarding this iconic figure, the name Cisero S. Murphy will never go unknown by any generation to come.

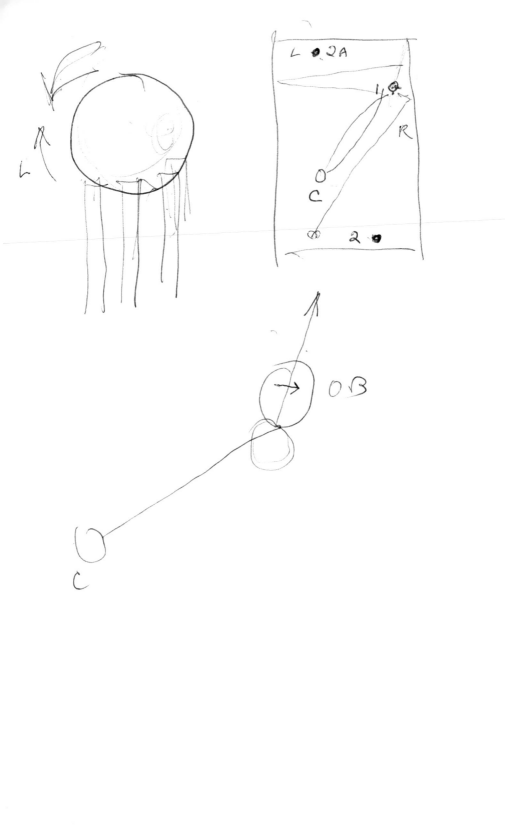

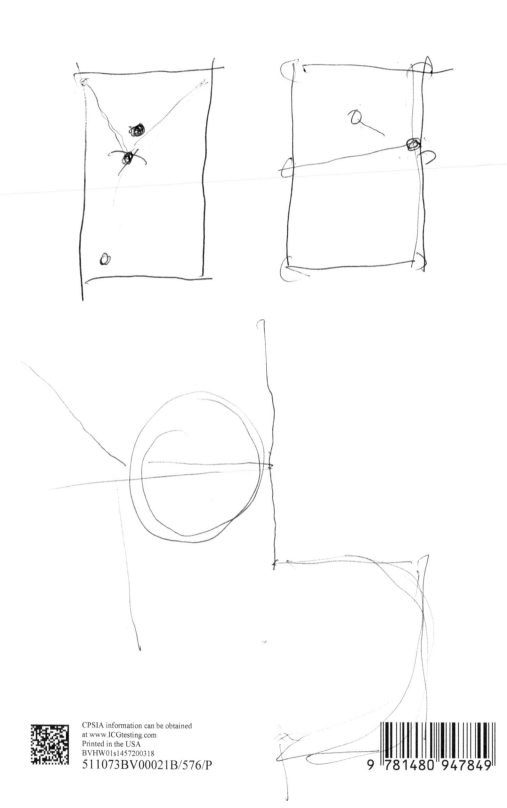

CPSIA information can be obtained
at www.ICGtesting.com
Printed in the USA
BVHW01s1457200318
511073BV00021B/576/P